I0060833

How To

Establish

Your Credit

Mark Kovach

Copyright: Pending

@2019 Mark Kovach All rights reserved

No part of this book may be reproduced, stored in a retrieval system, or transmitted by any means without the permission of the author.

ISBN-13:978-0-578-53681-1

Dedication

I would like to dedicate this book to Joan, my wife, the most wonderful lady, lover, friend, companion, and soul mate a man could ever ask for in this world. Joan has been my inspiration over the years and without her constant nagging at me, in a very nice way, I would have never finished this book, nor the other books that I had started years ago that was designed to teach everyone about the inter-workings of home buying and what mortgage loans are good and which ones are bad and need to be avoided at all costs, and is entitled *"Home Buying and Financing 101" now in its Second Edition, and "How Anyone Can Retire Living Large on Pennies," and "Making Parenting Simple, A Parenting Guide Handbook," and "How to Establish Your Credit."* Mr. Kovach also has a master's degree in business administration with a major in business finance. He is a retired loan officer and he and his wife enjoy a carefree lifestyle in Texas. Joan has been there by my side encouraging and motivating me and she has been my best helper, and companion throughout the years I have been writing these couple of books. Also, I would like to extend a very special thank you to the two most wonderful children a man could ever ask for, and they are my son Lance and my daughter Sherrell. Both of my kids are grown now, but nevertheless, they have been great contributors to all of my books even though they did not realize it because I had learned so much from them as they were growing up with Joan and me. I just want to thank Joan, Lance, and Sherrell for all their contributions, and the patience they had to endure over the years while growing up with me, and to let all of you know how proud I am to have them as my family.

Contents

Introduction

I have been a Loan Officer in the real estate business for many years and you get to meet all sorts of people. One such encounter happened back in the 80's when by accident I walked through a bank loan officer's door without knocking. When the door opened, here was this guy throwing wiffle ball darts at a dart board that was covered in velcro, and depending on where the wiffle dart landed he would take the file in front of him and either put it on the right or left side of his desk. When this guy turned around, you could tell by his facial expression that I was not the one who he had been expecting. This bank loan officer, (we will call Joe) turned out to be the bank's Branch Manager of a major bank in California and its Commercial Lending Officer. Nevertheless, I introduced myself and told Joe that I was interested in learning the in's and out's of the bank's real estate loan division, and how they determine who they will accept and who they will not accept as loan prospects that were interested in buying a home.

To make a long story short, Joe and I became very close friends over the years, and when I asked him what he was doing with the wiffle darts, he said he was the bank's Loan Committee who determined who would and who would not be granted a real estate loan from his particular bank. According to Joe, he had a wiffle ball dart system and depending on where the wiffle dart landed on the wiffle target, the people's home loan files were either stamped approved or denied. So, the real estate application files were then placed on the right of Joe's desk for funding or on the left side of his desk for the turndown real estate loans, and that is how Joe ran this bank when it came to real estate loans.

Joe had spent fifteen years in the banking business and was a member of The American Institute of Banking. This is a great organization that functions as the educational arm of banking. A large part of banking education is bankers teaching other bankers. This is greatly needed as the banking industry is constantly changing every day. More importantly, is the fact that this knowledge has been omitted from teaching the basic concepts of credit and banking to the American people.

Throughout this writing, I will offer some of Joe's helpful suggestions and scenarios we talked about, along with my real estate banking experience input that will assist the reader to become familiar, and, to get a better understanding of banking credit. Both Joe and I have noticed that most bank customers do not know the people in the banks or how to use the banks to their advantage. Our hope is that this writing will assist you in establishing and expanding your credit needs with a better understanding of what bankers are looking for in establishing basic credit.

SECTION 1

HOW TO ESTABLISH YOUR CREDIT

People in Banking

For years, the banking profession has been held in esteem in regard to integrity, honesty, and intelligence. When one looks at the people in their community, one will generally find a banker. However, in the past three or four decades the respectability has given way to negative publicity that some banks and bankers have given to the profession. Most of this negative publicity occurred during the financial meltdown in the early part of the year of 2008 and is still causing problems all because of the greed by the banking institutions. Nevertheless, the banking industry will continue to feel the ripple effects of this bad publicity for some time to come in the future.

In today's modern society one has to realize that a banker does not have the ability to be a total banker as it is an impossibility. In today's society the banking industry is far more sophisticated and complex than it has been in years past. With the proliferation of the computers there has been a development of several new positions that have opened up in the banks. Likewise, banking is world wide and requires knowledge concerning international finance, money transfer, etc. Along with this, major banks have trust departments offering several specialized services that requires numerous positions of various skills. Therefore, since we are in an age of specialization, banks can no longer afford to be total bankers.

Usually, people progressed through a career in banking starting in the bookkeeping department for a few years, then worked their way up into the lending and management areas. This was acceptable until the 1960s when the industry began expanding at a very rapid rate. Bankers then started looking around and found that there were very few qualified people coming into the banking profession and there wasn't sufficient time to train these new people. Some of the major banks started formal management programs to advance the new employees to fill these new positions. This is where one of the major banking dilemmas started. A new employee would be trained and then placed into a position after two years under someone who took 25 years to attain that same position. We have often heard, how long term employees would grumble and complain, "It took me 20 years to reach that salary level and I will not recommend him." At that time the industry had a lot of this thinking going on in the late 50's and 60's.

It should also be pointed out, even in specialized fields, that it could take several years of maturity to achieve total knowledge in one's area of expertise. Now that we have moved into the 21st Century, we find an industry that is replete with three types of employees: the bright young person who is eager to learn but does not have the time or experience needed to be successful. Next, we have the individual who for some unknown reason has been elevated to a position which is beyond their maximum potential. Lastly, we have that person who is very good and becomes a competent banker.

Here I would like to acquaint you with whom you are usually going to be dealing with when you walk into the majority of banks in America. According to my friend Joe he indicates and admits that the aforementioned stated above will cover the majority of people in the banking business even today. Joe had worked as a banker for over 15 years, and according to him, there was only one person in the Midwest who could be called a total banker. It is also interesting to note that this person did not go to college and had no degrees. Nevertheless, we have all met this type of individual who excels at anything they set out to do.

As we stated previously, it is important to get to know your banker. Likewise, you should get to know the proper people in your bank. What we have observed over the years is that the majority of bank customers only get to know the tellers. However, it is imperative that you get to know the president or vice president and the bank manager in your bank. Even if you have to go out of your way and take some extra time to do so. The goal here is to make a positive introduction and don't introduce yourself with a complaint like why did the bank not honor my check?

The next thing you want to do is to analyze the type and size of the banking system. If you reside in a state that has branch banking, be sure to get to know the branch manager and/or the assistant branch manager. If you decide to open an account, ask to be introduced to the managers and don't be embarrassed about the size of the account you are opening as this is the best time to be meeting the manager. Likewise, the manager will not know the size of your account and if he/she finds out later that your account is a small account, he/she will view your potential rather than the actual amount that you invested in the bank at that time. Nonetheless, if you think or feel that you are not meeting the right person, then we suggest that there are other banks you can go to that have and offer the same services. Remember, banking is a business and if you are not satisfied, don't hesitate to change banks.

Now, once you think or feel that you have met the proper person, be sure to say something positive. If you are young and new to the world of banking, ask the manager if you can stop by for some advice every now and then. If you are in college, tell them you are doing a paper and would appreciate getting their thoughts on a given subject. Furthermore, if you are already established in a profession or working situation, ask for some future advice that is related to what you are doing. By doing these simple things, you are meeting the right people and establishing follow-up conversations. Moreover, you are placing yourself in the bankers mind. Be sure when you come into the bank that you wave at these people and if they are not busy, stop by for a friendly hello. However, don't make a nuisance of yourself, but let them know that you are their customer.

Should your bank be one of the many smaller independent banks throughout America, you should do exactly the same thing. After you have opened your account or accounts, get to know one of the loan officers and stop by to say hello and follow the same procedures you would have in a branch bank. Here, too, you could make an appointment to meet one of the senior officers for an interview concerning your paper. Likewise, for the established worker or business man/woman you, too, can meet the same banking personnel, but don't hesitate to ask questions related to your business or profession and how it fits into the current economy. Ask the banker for his/her opinion on the economy and how it's trending. Remember, bankers are people, too, and they like to feel that they are on top of the current economic events and they will be honored to give you some excellent advice.

On the other hand, if you are doing business with one of the larger banks in America that has no branches, then most of their loan officers will be located on other floors and in other departments in the bank. The nice thing about these banks is that they have personal banking officers who are able to help you with your beginning banking needs. However, most of them will have limited credit authority but they can assist you with establishing your initial credit up to a certain amount. Again, we can't stress enough on the importance of getting to know your banker, be it the president, vice president or managers. This process is not something that will happen overnight, but it takes time, may be a couple of years to develop a good relationship with the bank personnel, but it will be well worth it in the long run.

Learning to Use Your Bank

Over the years Joe and I found out that the majority of people do not know how to use the banks in America to establish their credit and fulfill their credit needs and requirements. We have noticed that the majority of people do not understand how banks work and how to go about establishing themselves with credit at an early age so that when they get older they will have all the credit they will need.

It was also interesting for us to note that a number of successful people in their chosen field did not understand the basic concepts of borrowing money or the extent of their financial capabilities. To some extent, the information and examples cited herein by Joe may seem common place, but to others the process of borrowing money and establishing credit has created a great deal of frustration and turmoil and has been a source of great concern in the banking industry. One common situation that Joe and I have encountered over and over again is the solid young customer who is being turned down on a credit request because they were too new on their job or they did not have an established past credit background. We will try to show you how you can acquire a credit background so that by the time a person is in their early twenties they will have established banking credit. We also know that having a proven past banking credit background is a very positive fact on anyone's credit report.

The educational system in America is good at teaching theory, but a practical application of facts on banking and how they work is never offered. We both feel especially strong on this point when it comes to the medical profession. Here is a very skilled group of people who have a high degree of intelligence, but have a difficult time managing their own monies. It would be extremely worth while if the colleges would offer a course on basic banking practices for all professions and especially the medical profession. It would also be helpful if the high schools would offer a course on basic banking practices, specifically, on how to balance checkbooks and what to look for in reconciliation of a bank checking account.

We want to give the reader some insight that will make you more aware of what goes on in a bank and how it can benefit you. The following points will be important by indicating the things that will be needed for you to establish a good financial beginning at the bank of your choice. Over the years we have seen several interesting situations develop with customers.

We also know from our observance of people and their financial needs that approximately 90% of all the people do not understand how credit works and how they can establish themselves so they will have a proper credit background in order to help them expand their own personal financial goals. We would also like to point out some of Joe's actual cases of customers he has worked with over the years. Each of these cases will point out how most people do not understand how money works and where to acquire it at the lowest cost.

Several years ago Joe told me he was approached by a couple in their mid 50's in a Midwestern bank. These people were part of a growing and expanding computer firm and both of them worked in the math department. During this time they lived in a nice suburban home and were able to sell their home for $26,000.00 of which they only owed $6,000.00. The couple had a gross income of $30,000.00 a year. They had just found their dream home in another suburban community and were about to enter into a real estate sales agreement to purchase this home for 38,000.00. This was a very dramatic experience for this couple, and they were requesting a new 1st mortgage on the property of $18,000.00, and were concerned as to whether they would qualify for the loan. In today's housing market we would assume the above would sound even to the least knowledgeable on credit as quite a solid situation, but we must realize the time was in the late 60's before everything went crazy in the real estate market.

Joe asked the couple to fill out a financial statement and it showed that the couple owned over $180,000.00 of stock in their company. Because the company was growing so fast and was only able to pay stock dividends after it had split five times, they did not realize that they had such a large amount of equity in their company. Needless to say, the couple received their loan and when they found out they had excess income, two years later they paid the $18,000.00 1st mortgage loan off in full. What was interesting here is we have two very talented people having PH D's in mathematics and computer mathematical probability solving for their company, but they were totally unaware of their own personal financial capabilities and how to use it to their advantage.

In another situation that Joe and I discussed was a bank customer who had approached Joe for a small commercial loan to help him expand his business. This customer was forty-six years old and had recently gone through a divorce that turned out to be a true 50-50 split, where he received fifty percent of the liabilities and she received fifty percent of the assets. Nevertheless, in the divorce there was one liability he failed to pay that was a hundred and fifty dollars charge account at a major department store. When he found out about the bill a year and a half later he paid the bill off, but the girl at the counter told him that his credit was ruined forever. Years later this guy remarried and purchased a home for cash and never requested any credit and always paid everything in cash. When this person approached the bank Joe realized that it took a lot of courage for this guy to come into a bank to see a loan officer. As this guy was making his loan request, everything was done in a very professional manner for the first part of his request. However, he then began to tell Joe about the hundred and fifty dollars that was a past due charge account at a major department store, which he paid off when he found out about the charge. The funny thing about this situation was that by the time Joe was about finished with the loan papers this guy was ready to turn himself down for the loan. It is interesting to note just how many people do not have a positive attitude and are ready to turn themselves down on their own loan request. Nevertheless, Joe told this guy to stop talking and let him do the talking and explained to him the necessary information the bank would need in order to make a credit decision, and to let Joe advise him about his past credit and how it would affect the credit decision.

It was interesting to note that after checking this guy's credit report background the paid off hundred and fifty dollar charge off never showed up on his credit report. Since then he had maintained a thousand dollar average balance at the bank (later we will explain how this can work to your advantage) and had paid all his fixed payments on time. Also, you may not realize it but even without credit you still have some fixed payments of utilities, property taxes, etc. This guy's new wife had been employed for five years at the same position and his three-year-old company had shown excellent growth. This person was granted his loan for his business and it enabled him to expand adding four more employees. The loan was structured for a three-year loan payoff that was paid off in six months. The forgoing may have sounded like a large credit request, but it was for only a $5,000.00 loan. In this situation here was a good honest person who had one small misgiving about his past and for over seven plus years he felt he was unworthy of credit. The nice thing about this was he sold his mobile home for $45,000.00, and used it for a down payment on a large home, and we were able to give him a mortgage loan commitment for his new home.

We have one more example to relate to the reader and it is about a person who was not a customer at Joe's bank at the time. Joe's bank was approached by a loan company to purchase some of the trust deed loans that it held. At random Joe pulled out one of them and once again we noticed an example that reconfirmed our belief that most people do not understand credit and how or where to acquire it. Here was a person wanting a second mortgage on his personal residence having a first mortgage of $62,000.00 and was requesting a $25,000.00 second mortgage. The home had appraised for $230,000.00 and according to this person's tax returns. he had an adjusted gross income of over $120,000.00 for the last four years. He had been banking at one of the major banks in America and maintained a nice savings account there. At the loan company they had arranged a loan for him at the prime rate plus seven percent at a cost of a 10 point charge. At the time of this person's approval he received the $25,000.00 loan at twenty-one percent for three years at a cost of $2,500.00 in points and his net proceeds were less than $22,500.00. The interesting point here is that this guy's bank was making the same type of loan at 15.5 percent over twenty years at a cost of only 1 point or $250.00 in loan fees.

Many potential customers would qualify at a bank, but they never think of ever asking their own bank. This is a case of an individual who went to the bank every week to deposit his check and never took the additional time to ask a loan officer if they made second mortgage loans. In this situation the extra time would have saved this person $2,250.00 in loan fees and a lot of interest. There are a few people that you should know on a first name basis: Your doctor, dentist, druggist, banker, and service station owner or operator. Over the years we have had several people stop by once a week or so to just say hello. After a while you get to know this person and when credit gets tight or a situation develops, we can guarantee you it's a lot easier to get a loan. Again, the point being made is get to know your banker.

Standard Banking Operations

There are a few basic operational procedures everyone should understand even though there has been several books and manuals written on the subject. There are also some very important things one needs to do to help themselves establish their credit and personal financial future. Some of what we will be saying you may already know, but you should realize the importance of everything. Remember when we were talking about your checking account? When it is handled the right way, it can become a good tool to help you obtain the credit you want or need.

Here are some things most customers don't know: It is important that you know the cut off time at your bank or branch for that day's credit to be applied to your account. Several banks are open until 5 p.m., but their cut off time is 3 p.m. What this means is, if you make a deposit or cash a check before 3 p.m., it will show up on your balance that day. On the other hand, if a transaction is made after 3 p.m., it will not be posted to your account until the next banking business day because the bank computers will consider the transaction to have been made the following day.

For clarification let's view a very common situation where the husband is receiving his paycheck on Friday and he will deposit it at the bank before he comes home.The wife goes out and does her shopping knowing that today is payday. Now, most businesses know that if they deposit before 3 p.m., they will get an extra day's credit in their checking accounts. However, the store where the wife purchased her morning groceries at 2 p.m. and the employed husband stops by the bank to make his deposit at 5 p.m. on his way home, both the husband and wife feel that since everything was done the same day that there will be no problem. Technically, the husband and wife are right, but in the real world of banking they are a day late. What happens is that the next day the bank computer prints out an overdraft and their overdraft is recorded in the computer. Hopefully, this will be the husband and wife's first overdraft and they have been customers a long time, in which case the bank will try to call them. In the event contact is not made, their check(s) will probably be returned with a service charge.

There are two points we want to make here. The first is, if you never write a check before you make a deposit you will never be in trouble. The second one is, if you do write a check(s) and you are at the bank to make your deposit, be sure to tell the teller to mark the journal showing your deposit. Doing this will not insure your protection, as new journals come out the next day, but this procedure should help prevent most same-day problems.This is why it is important to remember to balance your bank statements. Learning how to do this in the correct way will assist you in the event you might have any question concerning your account. You can also go to your bank and they will be more than happy to assist you with the proper format. In addition, there are other very important things to remember concerning your monthly statements. Your monthly statement will show a final date of the monthly activity on your account and at the same time showing you the balance in your account as of that date. When you are balancing your account that is the date you work with in your checkbook. Let's say the date of the statement is June 30, but you received your statement on July 11, look at your checkbook register and balance it as of June 30. You will be concerning yourself with checks and deposits made on June 30 or prior. The checks after June 30 will be in your following month's statements. If everything is okay you should have a higher bank statement balance than in your checkbook and that is due to the float factor between your writing checks and when they reach your bank to be paid.

The majority of people do not take the time each month to balance their checkbooks and check to see if they have made a subtraction or an addition error. Because of the float factor you may not show an overdraft, but in the long run it will catch up with you. Therefore, it is vitally important that you balance your checkbook with the bank statement every month. Another crucial situation that is overlooked is to write down each check or debt card purchase in your checkbook register when you write a check and keep an accurate running balance. This may sound like common sense, but it is one of the major areas where people get themselves into trouble.

It may be embarrassing for you while you are at the grocery store to record the check you have just written and subtract out the balance right there at the counter, because there is a big line behind you, and you say that you will remember to do this when you get home. If you only knew how many times people have come to the bank all upset because they received an overdraft notice because they forgot to include the check for $79.95 at the grocery store in their register. They generally come into the bank with the attitude that the bank is wrong. However, after gathering the customer's checks, we ask them how they balanced their last statement and they usually respond by saying it was correct. Next, we ask to see their checkbook register and we usually see that there is no running balance and there are lines running all over the place. It may take several minutes, but we are able to see where most of the checks have a place and then to your customer's amazement, there is the check for $79.95 that's not in their checkbook, which told the computer that the account is overdrawn. By this time the customer who stormed into the bank in total anger and frustration is now very meek and feeling rather foolish.

The situation we really like is where the one spouse comes storming into the bank saying that the bank has made a mistake on their husband's or wife's account. In the majority of situations like this it eventually relates back to one of them not recording a check. Joe related to me where he remembers a man who came storming up to his desk using very bad language. After Joe had gone through this guy's checks, Joe found one check that was not recorded in the register for $300.00 and marked for a new dress for his wife. He then apologized and went out looking for his wife. Needless to say we never did learn what happened after that, but it is fair to assume that he had some serious conversation with his wife that night. The main point we are making here is to record your checks, otherwise an overdraft will be recorded in the computer and will not help you in your request for credit independence.

Furthermore, we do not want to sound like the great defenders of the banking system, but in the case of overdrafts the bank is correct 99% in all situations. So, in the event you have an unpleasant experience of receiving an overdraft notice, realize before you run to the bank that the odds are against you and check your records thoroughly. On the other hand, if you still do not find or see where an error was made, approach the bank in a calm way and you will be surprised with a more positive response.

What's important to remember is that the bank's computer can only read the numbers on the bottom of the check. After you receive your bank statement, you will see in the lower-right hand corner of the check is encoded the amount of the check you have written. This is the amount that the computer will charge your account. It is here that banks will make the largest percentage of mistakes. Let's say you wrote a check for $150.00, but in the lower right corner it shows 240.00. You now know that was the amount charged to your account. Now, before you run to the bank and give them a piece of your mind, look on the back of your check to see what bank the check was deposited in as that was the bank where the error occurred; that bank will then credit your bank and your account, and you do not go to that bank, but rather to your bank.

The bank will take care of the necessary corrections. An example: let's say that you bank at bank X and you purchased some clothes from Jackie's clothing store and Jackie makes a deposit at bank Z, and it is Jackie's bank that encodes the wrong figure. This figure will go through the banking system with that figure until you notice it in your statement. Due to the fact that thousands of checks are being processed daily, it would be extremely rare that your bank would catch this mistake. Again, the point we are making here is to take care of your checking account in the correct way as that is one of the tools that will help you establish credit.

What Bankers Want to See

The question of what do bankers want to see is relatively simple because banks want deposits and the more checking account deposits, the better. This makes sense because checking account deposits, known as demand accounts, are the cheapest accounts for the banks. These accounts help you when you are applying for a loan. Banks take into consideration your account relationship when they quote you an interest rate on a loan, and the larger your average checking account balance, the better your loan interest rate should be.

Likewise, we understand how it is nice to have an account at a thrift institution because you do receive a higher rate of interest on your money, but when and if you ever need a bank loan, you will also end up paying a higher interest rate to borrow money for whatever loan amount you require. If you use a figure of twenty percent free compensating balances, you can figure on a lower interest rate. What we are talking about here is, let's say that you have an average checking balance of $2,500.00 and are requesting a loan of $15,000.00, you might get one or two percent off on the interest rate because of your balance relationship with the bank. This then is important for customers who are requesting or need larger loan amounts as you will receive more consideration for any savings accounts you have at the bank. In other words, due to the cost of funds factor your interest rate break will not be as great, but it could outweigh any differences you would get by having your monies in a thrift institution. Just remember that a compensating balance is the amount of money you have on deposit at your bank and the amount of your outstanding loans.

We know of some customers who would tell us, "Well, we purchased Treasury Bills through this bank," but outside of a small fee to cover the paper work the benefits of a Treasury Bill goes to the United States Government and not to the bank. Also, having a safe deposit box at a bank will not get a banker to notice you for a favorable interest rate loan. Safe deposit boxes are nothing more than a convenience being offered by banks and is one of the areas of a bank that makes very little money for the bank.

Another important subject to remember is just to be yourself when you visit your banker and not to attempt to oversell yourself by overdressing or dressing up. Over the years we have seen several kinds of dress, but the ones who overdress to impress their banker do not make a very good impression. We don't mean to imply you should spend your day in curlers and that it is proper to dress that way for a loan request appointment. The same applies to people who work in a dirty work environment as it doesn't hurt to clean up a little, but just be yourself.

Years ago Joe told me about a customer who came into the bank and he looked like he just came from a farm. As Joe started to approach this person he could tell the guy was frustrated. When Joe asked the guy if he could be of some help, he said yes and thank you. As it turned out this guy just came from the bank across the street and they had asked this guy to leave because he happened to track in some mud. As it turned out, Joe opened a savings account that day for this guy in the amount of eighty-thousand dollars. So, as anyone can now see, looks can be very deceiving, so just be yourself.

The Beginning of Credit

A lot of young people hear the same old cliche, "We are sorry but you cannot purchase this furniture, car, home, or etc., because you don't have any established credit." This is a typical situation that is repeated over and over again all across the United States. However, the people being turned down has nothing to do with their character or their trust worthiness because it docs take time to establish a person's credit, therefore, our advice is to give yourself time by starting while you are young. Here is an example: When you go to a bank to ask for a loan for whatever reason and you are new on your first job and even though you have a good income, you will probably be turned down for a loan. The reason banks do this is because you do not have a credit background and should the bank decide to issue you a loan, they will require that you have a co-signer. What the bank is trying to tell you here is that they do not know if you will have the ability or stability on your job to set fixed funds aside each month to pay the loan back on time. Nevertheless, time will remedy this situation.

Banks like secured loans and those secured by savings accounts in their own bank or branch make them even happier. What you need to understand is that when banks lend you money that is secured by your own account, they are required by law to charge you at least one percent over the rate they are paying you on your account. All banks are different and some will charge you two or three percentage points over the rate they are paying you, but regardless of what it is, it is a reasonable price for you to pay. There is also the fact that the banks have minimum loan fees that can be anywhere from one hundred dollars and up depending on the particular bank.When you are applying for a loan, go into your bank and request to borrow a thousand dollars and tell your banker that you want these funds deposited into a savings account against the loan you're requesting. The banker will be pleased to hear this as their degree of exposure on the loan is the interest rate factor. When the loan is approved, ask that it be set up on monthly payments for twelve months or for a period of time that your monthly income can support. Now, during the time your loan is in effect you are accomplishing two things. First of all you are proving to your banker that you can set aside the proper amount every month to pay your monthly obligations. Secondly, you are now building a savings account and as long as you reduce your loan balance the equity in your savings account grows. Once you pay off your loan in full ask the bank to notify the major credit bureaus as this will then be your first positive indication of credit on your record, which will show that you had a secured loan that was paid as agreed. However, we need to point out here that a lot of credit bureaus will not show or indicate that the loan was a savings account loan.

To further establish and extend your credit background, we would recommend that you ask your banker to loan you some money for a period of ninety days, once again, use your savings account as security for the loan. Be prepared to pay off your loan around the eighty-fifth or eighty-ninth day and never go over the ninety-day time limit. The eighty-fifth and eighty-ninth day is important because most bank computers will send you a statement of how much you still owe about two weeks before your loan is due. Likewise, the officer that loaned you the money will also receive a computer report about ten days before your loan is due and your name and credit report will be fresh in his mind. Furthermore, when you go into the bank to pay your loan off, be sure to stop by the loan officer and tell him why you are at the bank. This is important because you are letting the loan officer know that you are around even though you may know where the note department is in the bank, but let the loan officer tell you where it is. Consequently, the loan officer is getting to know you and you are letting him know that you have paid your loan off in full.

At this time you might be thinking that you do not make enough money to pay off your loan at the specified time. However, you might have a side venture that you are expecting a return on and you could indicate this expected income at the time you are making your ninety-day loan. It would be advisable to take those funds and leave them in your checking account over this period of time. We do not recommend that you add these funds to your savings account in this instance because it would not be that beneficial. Let the banker think that you used the loan for this specified business venture as it is from that venture that the source of repayment is coming from to pay off your loan obligation. By this time you should be in your twentieth month, plus or minus a few months, working with your banker during which time your checking account has been handled correctly and you have maintained at least a hundred dollar average balance with no overdraft notifications. You also have two loans with your bank and you have proven that you can generate the monies required to pay off any loans you have had with the bank. As long as your loan request is commensurate with your income level, this then becomes a very valid and important point at your bank. The next step is to approach the bank for a loan that is about half of your savings balance. Let's say that would be around five hundred dollars and again ask for a ninety-days loan, but this time, ask that the loan be unsecured. Even though this may cause some trouble, as a lot of banks don't care to have such small loans on their books for only a ninety-day period. There is also the minimum loan charge that banks require that is to be taken into consideration and the annual percentage rate on the loan may shock you. Nevertheless, the one thing for you to remember is that the minimum loan charge and the increased interest rate is allowing you the opportunity to increase your credit status with the bank. In this situation the bank may not offer you a ninety-day note in which case you can ask them if you can have a reserve line on your checking account for this period of time. If the bank agrees the reserve line will usually be a one time advance and the account will be frozen until it is paid in full.

Another way to do this is to ask the bank to issue a Visa or Master Charge account under a one time advance, and you don't even have to concern yourself that the bank even issuing you a card at this time. However, when the loan is paid you will have shown the bank and banker that you are a responsible person. During this time you have gotten to know your banker and the people they work with and you have demonstrated your abilities to satisfy your bank loan obligations thereby establishing a good credit report.

If you have established credit in only one location with only one bank and you happen to move to another area, find a bank you like and then go back to the bank you just left where you established your credit and ask the banker if they would write you a letter of reference. Note that this is very important because people tend to move around in the US a lot and are required to reestablish their credit background in a new area. On the other hand, if you are staying with the bank where you now have established credit, it's time to ask for some additional credit. Ask for a Visa or Master Card or a reserve line of credit on your checking account and you can also ask for an applications for gas cards. More than likely you will be turned down on some of your applications, but make enough of them and you will receive some. If and when you use these cards, be sure to use them to make at least one small purchase and when you receive the statement, pay it immediately, then put the card away someplace where you can't use it. The reason for this is that gas credit cards can and will get used over and over again to the point that you will not be able to get out from under them and their fees, and eventually they will end up destroying your credit history.

Over the years we have assisted many young people in establishing their credit backgrounds using the same techniques mentioned above. Likewise, some of these people were able to acquire loans up to as much as ten thousand dollars unsecured by the time they were in their early twenties. Remember, establishing credit is not hard, but it will take some time.

How to Expand Your Credit

Granted it is important to establish a solid foundation in one's credit background, but it is also important to understand and to know how to expand one's credit and yet not to expand it too much by getting one's self into financial trouble. We can't begin to tell you how many times we have heard people say, "These darn credit cards make it so easy to make purchases." Well, the fact is that these people are correct and it is not very easy for people to stop using credit cards. People need to learn how to discipline themselves and not try to expand their credit too fast and, yes, we know, it is easier said than done. The banks along with the large retail markets are causing these problems because they make it easy for people to get all the credit cards they want and then the large retail market along with the credit card companies are constantly encouraging the people to use their credit cards. The purchase now and pay later philosophy has gotten out of hand in our today's society. It's okay to use your credit card for some major purchases, but sooner or later it will get away from people if they are not careful.

Add up all your fixed monthly payments including your mortgage or rent payments, car payments, and any other term payments that you have more than three months of remaining payments. Once you come up with a figure take your gross income and divide it into the total of your payments and you'll get a percentage figure. Should your figure exceed forty-five percent, you need to restrict your credit purchases immediately as you are walking a fine line of getting yourself into serious financial trouble. For your information the banks use your gross income in the above explanation, but since your gross income doesn't belong to you, we use net income figures that are the real figures that you should be looking at because these figures will keep you from getting into a financial situation that you will have a hard time getting out of if you can. It has been proven over and over again that once you exceed forty-five percent of your gross income that your chances of going bankrupt increase at a very rapid rate. On the other hand, using your net income to get to the forty-five percent figure will usually stop this from becoming a reality. Example: Let's say that your gross income is $5,000.00 a month and 45% of that would be $2,250.00 you could have in monthly maximum outgoing retail payments. Now, let's use your net income, (which the author of this book has always used) using the same figures above, you get $5,000.00 minus 25% which comes to $1,250.00 dollars that you again subtract from the $5,000.00 gross income, and your net income is now $3,750.00 minus 45% comes to $2,062.50 leaving you a margin of $187.50 or enough room to stay out of trouble providing you stop spending until you can pay down your balance.

Naturally, there are exceptions to the rules, but the largest percentage of people will find themselves in a very tight financial situation should they reach this forty-five percent figure based on their gross income. Using your net income figure at the same forty-five percent figure will let you know that you are getting close to being in financial trouble, yet far enough away that you can get out of trouble by curbing your spending habits until you can pay down the balance and then you can start again if you have more to purchase.

Joe related another story to me that involved a young couple in California who were at a seventy-five percent retail figure based on their gross income, but managed to pull things together and get out of trouble. The only reason this couple made it out of trouble was that for three years they both worked night and day to establish their own business and to eventually payoff all of their bills. They now have a very successful business and are able to relax. There is also the situation where your gross income increases and your margins left over increases, but remember from your gross income comes your Federal and State Taxes along with other deductions, which is the difference between this figure and the forty-five percent figure that you have to cloth and feed and support your family. Otherwise known as your net income. That is why the author of this book has always used the net income figure and has never gotten himself into financial trouble. In the above discussion, by using your net income figure you should never get any closer than eight to ten percentage points away from the forty-five percent figure. Furthermore, if you reach this point, one should take a very close look at their spending habits and adjust them. It is also a lot easier to adjust your spending habits than it is to expand your income. On the other hand, should you be using your gross income figure and you start approaching the forty percent figure, people need to take a very serious look at your spending habits and adjust them as you are heading for financial trouble and possible bankruptcy. People need to realize that with the high cost of housing and interest rates the banks no longer look at the old ratios of the past. In the area of real estate lending we used to look at principal, interest, taxes, and insurance that were not to exceed twenty-five percent of your monthly income. There was also a rule we followed that indicated that we use two and a half times your yearly income, which was the maximum home a person could afford at that time. Nevertheless, with the rapid increase in the housing market over the last few decades our lending ratios increased to a standard of 28/36 percent (read as 28 over 36 in the loan industry) indicating more leeway for homebuyers. However, as home pricing continued to increase lenders would go as high as 33/45 percent providing the borrower had a good credit background.

What this all means is that we are now going be using more of our net income to cover the basic cost of housing. This is what people have been doing in other countries for decades. Moreover, this leaves us with a lesser percentage between our housing cost and the limit to which we can expand our credit. It also indicates that in the future more and more people will get into severe financial difficulties because they will be expanding their credit way too fast. We have also heard people indicate that it is cheaper to purchase an item now as it will be paid back in cheaper dollars. This may be true to a certain point, but by purchasing this item today, one is pushed over the forty-five percent bracket, then the people should be prepared for some serious financial problems. Granted it might be cheaper to purchase the item today, but wait until you have the cash to pay for the item.

Small Business Credit

If a small or medium size business decides to approach a bank for a loan request it is important that they do it in an appropriate way. There have been several times that loan applications have been submitted to banks and once a loan officer analyzes the information, he states, "Who are they trying to fool?" It's not like the loan officer is turning you down or indicating that your business loan request is not needed. They are simply looking at the facts as presented in your application and the facts do not add up. There are several small things you can do to make sure your facts are being presented in the correct way. Usually, small businesses will try to do their own bookkeeping or hire a service so you can see exactly where you are at the end of each month. Once you have reached a certain business volume you will usually expand to a public accountant and then to a certified public accountant. When you receive your financial statement, make sure you understand everything in the statement. There is one thing here that we will point out, which is that your tax returns for the business agree with your business statement. If it does not agree, then an explanation needs to be indicated in the footnotes. In the event a business is a corporation there will be an area in your tax returns where you can adjust the business statement to your tax return. However, a business statement is rather self-explanatory when prepared by a certified public account. It is important to know that your personal financial statement be filled out with real figures that can be verified.

As far as stock is concerned there is a place in your statement to list your unlisted stock, but be careful as time and time again we have noticed some very distorted figures in this location. Okay, your financial statement on your business has your business showing a net worth of $75,000.00 and where it indicates your stock, assuming you own one hundred percent of your business stock be sure to put the $75,000.00 in this area. As funny as it may seem, we have seen figures in excess of a half a million dollars to be used as the stock value and when it is compared with your business financial statement, we usually see figures 10 to 15 times smaller. We also realize that you could indicate your business is worth more than its net worth, but if you want to inflate the net worth, you need to use a figure that you can support. We have also seen businesses with net worths of a quarter of a million dollars that had offers over a million dollars from qualified buyers. Should you have something like this occur, then you can justify increasing the figure. Just make sure your financial statement makes sense and your figures can be supported. Another major area that gets blown out of proportion on a statement is real estate, and again it is important to use realistic values on real estate. Showing you purchased a home five months ago for $200,000.00 and now it's worth $250,000.00, you need to be able to justify the increase in value of your real estate. Granted there may be an explanation to the increased value of your property, but you need to be ready to explain and justify the reason for the increased value. Like we said before there are always exceptions to the rule and in this situation we had a customer's statement who indicated an initial land purchase for $50,000.00 dollars that she bought in March of a given year and in September of that same year she indicated the land was worth a little over three million dollars. Even the weakest of bankers would question and challenge this situation. As it turned out this customer was completely prepared and what she stated was all true. She had entered into an agreement several years prior from an estate and the estate agreed to sell her this land and her money was placed into an escrow account. It took several years for the estate to close and in March of that year she received fee titled to the land. There were several reasons for the delay of the estate and one of the reasons occurred about three years into the purchase of this land. As it turned out someone decided that this land would be the perfect site for a major baseball stadium. Needless to say, the estate also liked the idea and it took the buyer four years in court before she was finally authorized to go ahead with the purchase of the land as agreed in the contract for $50,000.00 dollars. In this situation it indicates that the land buyer knew she would probably have to answer questions concerning the land value and she saved a considerable amount of trouble having the land put into an escrow account as she had the answers when the time came.

Another area in your statement that you will need to justify is your personal property. This figure will comprise everything that was not included in your previous statement. Also, when it comes to silver, gold, diamonds, major furniture, and artworks that can constantly go up and down in value, be sure to list those values separately. Make sure you have these items appraised and you just might be surprised at the value these items will have. There is also a place on the financial statement to indicate your yearly income and be sure to indicate whether the income is taxable or not. This is another area where people will inflate their income as opposed to what they actually receive. A banker will request your last year's tax returns that should agree with what you state on your financial statement. In the event that these figures do not agree, then you need to be able to explain to the banker where you derived your income.

We have seen situations where the financial statement shows a $130,000.00 dollars in income and the tax returns show $30,000.00 dollars in adjusted gross income. Even though this may be correct, be sure to take your whole tax return to the bank so they can go back through your returns in order to justify your figures. This is very essential because you may have a lot of depreciation and your real cash flow may be a lot better than you have lead the banker to believe. On an on-going basis you should always continue to analyze and know your banking situation so that you can plan ahead for your business needs and requirements. Bankers don't like it when someone comes in and tells them that they needed the money yesterday. Even though this may sound strange, this situation happens all to often and unless you have established a strong relationship with your bank, you might just find yourself out in the street.

Learn and Know Your Bank's Limits

A bank's limitations are found in two areas, one being the services they offer and the other is how the lending structure works. It is imperative that you know in what areas in the lending field a bank places their emphasis on because you may be banking at the wrong bank for your business needs. Also, all banks advertise that they are full service banks because they offer many diversified services. However, even though this may be true, they may specialize in only a particular type of loan over others. There are certain banks that offer SBA loans, (Small Business Administration), but they will inform you right away that they do not make this type of loan. Other banks will stress that they make interim-construction loans, but not accounts receivables. Others will specialize in floating lines of credit and other banks do not care to make long term real-estate loans, yet they are very active in the home equity and home improvement loan areas.

This is why we stress that it is imperative that you understand the lending limits of your particular bank. If you are doing business with a bank that has a legal lending limit of two hundred and fifty-thousand dollars and you need five hundred thousand dollars or more in accounts receivables line of credit, then you need to evaluate your bank's situation, especially, if you plan to grow and be successful in your business. Granted the smaller bank will be able to do a five hundred thousand dollar account receivables credit line, but they will be working with other small banks or its major correspondent bank who shares in the loan. On the other hand, if you are dealing with larger banks, then it may not make any difference to you or your business. When selecting your bank, take a good hard look at your business and try to project and evaluate whether or not your business banking needs can be met by your bank in future years. The majority of people are already with proper banks, but there may be a few who need to analyze their expanding banking credit needs.

We often hear people tell us that they have been turned down by a bank's loan committee, which we find to be a very interesting statement as most of the time it is not a loan committee who turned your loan down, but rather it was the banker or his supervisor of the loan department who said no. The primary reason for this diversion tactic is that it makes it a lot easier for the banker to inform you that it was the bank's loan committee that turned you down as people are not inclined to question that decision. On larger loans or credit requests it just may be a loan committee who turns you down, but on loans or credit requests under $50,000.00 dollars, the person you were looking at and talking with turned you down or the person they report to for loan approval turned you down.

It is necessary to understand your bank's loan limits and how they work because the loan limit is the maximum amount established by a bank that their loan officers are able to lend to any one customer. The loan limit would also include all of the debt a customer would have with their bank. Let's say the branch manager had a loan limit of $30,000.00 dollars and your current loan debt with the bank is $15,000.00 dollars and you would like a loan to buy a vehicle for $25,000.00 dollars. Remember, the bank manager will know what kind of loans the bank wants along with the credit requirements they will expect. When the bank manager glances at your loan request and notices that it will not conform to the bank's requirements, he/she could technically turn you down right then. However, most of the time this will not happen even though the bank will not authorize the loan. Because the chances of you getting a loan are not good, he/she will tell you that they will get back to you in a couple of days. There are situations where the manager will not even present your loan request up the corporate ladder because they know their loan supervisor might question their abilities concerning the understanding of the bank's loan guidelines. Normally, you will get a call or a letter in a couple of days that will explain the reason why the bank's loan committee turned your loan request down. It is also highly unlikely that the bank will inform you that his/her supervisor turned you down or that there is no bank loan committee and that they did nothing with your loan application but run a credit report. The real fact of the matter is that you exceeded the bank's loan limit because the bank's loan limit was $30,000.00 dollars and with your current loan of $15,000.00 dollars and your new loan request for $25,000.00 dollars would take you to $40, 000.00 dollars, which would be $10,000.00 dollars over the bank's loan limit.

It, therefore, is crucial that you comprehend how the banking system functions so that you can submit your credit request with the knowledge of how the banks work. Like the situation mentioned above, once the bank manager gives his approval on the loan, the credit manager becomes responsible to his/her loan supervisor. The loan supervisor will only see you on paper and it is unlikely that you will ever meet this mystery person. One of the essential circumstances of a loan credit decision is the disposition of the person with whom we are dealing with that will never be revealed or show up on any paperwork, but as a bank manager we need to include this in our presentations. In the event that you have been turned down by your bank for a loan request, be sure to ask why you believe that the explanation being given is incorrect, and make sure that you elucidate that to your loan officer. There have been several loans at banks all across the United States where the persons requesting a loan were turned down and because of their strong will, these people were able to have their banker/loan officer change their minds.

There are several banks that have many different ways of establishing their lending authority, and we know of a couple of banks in California where the managers have the authority to manage about ninety percent of all their bank's loan requests. Smaller banks may make larger loan commitments and all banks have loan committees that are not usually used as much as people are led to believe. Some banks allow loan officers to merge their loan limits. In this circumstance you have two loan officers that each have a loan authority of $50,000.00 dollars and once merged they can make a loan of $100,000.00 dollars. There are additional banks that will let their loan officers loan up to half the bank's legal lending limit. Again it is vital that you learn that every bank is different in the area of substantiating loan authority. Usually, the branch or the bank manager will have the largest loan limit in the bank. Normally, in the independent banking system the senior loan officer or the president of the bank will have this lending authority. Correspondingly, there are extremely large banks that maintain large branch offices where the bank managers may have loan authority of up to a half a million dollars. That is why it is extremely necessary that you have the understanding of who you're dealing with and determine if that person is the correct person that can handle these kinds of loans that you may need now or in the future to come.

It Can Be Worth It to Shop Around

Is it likely for a small investor to survive it in today's world of high interest? The answer is a definite yes, but they need to be more aware of what is going on in the world of finance. People cannot expect to save a major percentage of their paycheck like they have in the past. Therefore, you have to ask yourself, when do you save it when inflation is on the rise? Likewise, when people are in need of a loan, they should shop around as you should do with everything else people would like, want, or need. It would also be smart to make several calls because you just might be amazed at the amount of savings you could get just talking to different people you're contemplating doing business with. All banks have interest rates, but different banks have different interest rates for different kinds of loans. Save yourself some money by simply calling different banks and asking what they would charge in interest rates for the type of loan you are interested in applying for. Also, don't forget to call your bank where you maintain your bank accounts as this will give you some leverage. Should you own your own business and maintain your business account at a different bank than your personal account, be sure to call that bank also.

Allow me to reiterate another story Joe related to me years ago. Joe knew of a businessman that was successful who he knew through an associate that wanted another car loan. Apparently, this person told Joe that he had gone to his bank where he had three previous vehicle loans and was quoted an interest rate of 19% simple interest. When Joe asked him if this was the same bank that he had his personal accounts at, this businessman said no. Joe then told him to call his bank and ask them what they could do concerning a car loan for him. Several weeks later the businessman called Joe back to inform him that he had gotten a five percent discount off the interest rate the other bank quoted him. Now, this may not sound like much, but for a new car financed for five years the interest rate savings would be considerable. Granted that the story we just related to you may not be a situation that you might get yourself into, but it happens over and over every day across America. However, the point being made is that if you take the time required to shop around, you can save yourself considerable money in financing.

When you are calling around for rates, be sure to ask if the loan will be simple interest or add-on interest. Simple interest installment loans will operate similar to a mortgage loan on your home and if you make a payment that is larger than your regular house payment, the difference will be applied to the principal that will reduce the principal balance of your home loan.

Furthermore, if the bank does not offer a simple interest installment loan program, they will be offering an add-on interest rate loan. This type of loan is where a bank figures the interest rate charges for the period of time of the loan and adds that to the principal amount borrowed and then divides that figure by the number of months you are requesting for your installment loan. Also, with the add-on interest loan, the bank will earn most of the interest charged back in the first part of the loan term. Therefore, if you decide to pay the loan off early, the amount of interest that you will get back will be less. On the other hand, with a simple interest rate installment loan, you will save yourself some interest back on the loan should you decide to pay off the loan prior to the loan's maturity date.

If or when one ever decides to get a home improvement loan, call your bank and the other banks located in your area and check to see what interest rates are along with the cost of the loan in points. Be sure to ask the bank if there will be any prepayment charges in the event you pay the loan off early. Note that several dealers also offer home improvement loans as they probably have made arrangements with different financial institutions, but their interest rates are usually higher than the interest rates the banks may be offering. Remember, that banks have several different and alternative loan programs all having variable service charges with the accounts, so be sure to check around your area to get the best interest rates being offered as you can save yourself a considerable amount of money. But, be aware that most banks who are offering overdraft lines of credit on a checking account will usually waive any service charges. Again, the banks can only charge you when you use your line of credit.

Most banks will charge you for checks, but it is reasonable even though the banks make a small profit. Banks do lose money on safe deposit box rentals, but they cannot afford to lose in other areas or they would go out of business. However, you should ask the bank what the minimum amount is required in a checking or savings account to wave all check fees and other bank charges. Again, all banks will have different fees in order to get free bank services on everything including free cashier or traveler checks. Some banks may require a minimum balance of five thousand, ten thousand, or as much as fifteen thousand dollars that must be maintained monthly in an account in order for people to be granted these free services. Again it doesn't make any difference what accounts these amounts are in as long as one meets the bank's minimum requirements. On savings accounts that are over one hundred thousand dollars, it pays to shop different banks as you may gain as much as one and a half or two percent more interest on your money. As we stated before it pays to shop around and this is true for any type of loan and be sure to call or stop by your bank when you are first starting out.

Things to Remember About Banks and Banking

The information we have put forth in this credit book will give anyone the tools and skills to start your credit and establish your credit background and eventually increase your credit in the future to meet or satisfy your needs. We have seen several different statistics that indicated that if a person only looked, they would have found what they were looking for in their own backyard. Look at your bank first and then begin looking at other banks, and if you don't like what you're hearing, or your bank doesn't offer you what you're looking for in the way of services try another bank. As a rule, banks will offer their customers most of the financial services that they will need, and usually, at a lower rate than if you used the services of another bank, but this may or may not be the case in your situation so shop around.

It is imperative that you get to know the appropriate people in the bank where you're doing business. It is also essential to remember that bankers have egos and you need to play on their egos. We also want to point out to people that bankers usually have more knowledge on the subject matter you may be discussing, but use general psychology and play on the banker's ego. Remember, introduce yourself in a positive way and let them know that you are or will be one of their customers. There may be a circumstance that comes up where your first introduction to a bank officer is due to a negative situation. In the event that this happens do not enter the bank with an attitude of I got you now, but rather show some consideration and turn the negative situation into a positive introduction. In this situation, the fact that you're showing self-restraint may save you several dollars at a later date when you may need some sort of credit.

The best way to begin your credit future is to maintain your checking account in the appropriate way and try to maintain a balance of at least a hundred dollars or more in your account at all times. Be careful that you do not write a check before you make a deposit and be certain to make sure the deposit is in the hands of the teller and recorded in the bank's computer. There are a massive amount of people today who bank with their computers online, but just because you use this method of banking, don't think that it is okay to start writing checks. Until your bank clears the deposit and it has been recorded into the bank's computer, you technically do not have a valid deposit.

Although some people get by with writing checks, they are basically counting on the float factor and they do not realize it or what they are doing. Unless you have a hundred percent confidence and trust that your bank has recorded your deposit in the bank's computer, just hold off for a day. Furthermore, you do not want to write a check before your bank's cutoff time for that day.

We have also discussed the information that is retained in the computer when your account is overdrawn. The computer also maintains information on any loans that you may have at the bank. Nonetheless, even though most people believe that they have ten days or so to make their payment or payments, they are considered past due by the bank's computer and the majority of the people believe they have thirty days before they are considered late or have a problem where they are banking. Normally, the bank's computer will not report you having a late payment on a loan until five days after the payment is past due assuming your loan was due on the first of the month. The next computer print out will be on the tenth of the month, and believe us, this is the one you do not want to have showing up on the computer readout. You may be asking yourself why this is so important and it is because banks will report this to the credit reporting agencies on how many ten-day late notices you have had and this will be reflected as derogatory credit on your credit report. Should your loan payment due date not correspond with your pay period or your pay period has been changed, go to your bank and ask them to change the due date on your loan or loans.

All the above information is critical because you definitely don't want any ten-day late notices showing up on your credit report. There may be times that you have told your loan officer that you will be late with a loan payment thinking that it will be okay and the loan officer responds saying that it will be okay. Granted, the loan officer will mark a reporting sheet in front of you. Then at the loan officers meeting they will make their reports, but what they don't tell you is that they do not change the bank's computer memory, and sitting in the bank's computer is the ten-day late reported on your record. So, when your loan is paid in full and reported to the credit agencies, someone in their backroom who has never seen your file will pull your information from the computer and report only that which the computer has stored in it. The point being made is to make your payments on time or ask the bank to change your due date. Also, make sure and ask that they can have the computer not indicate the late payment.

When you are establishing credit, make sure your introduction is positive, and yes, we know that we are being repetitive, but it is essential that you make a good rememberable impression with the right people. Since there are several thousands of banks all across the US, you can be selective even though the majority of people look for a bank out of convenience. Even though you may have to go a little out of your way, the rewards you will receive can be more than worth it. In reference to venture capital loans, note that banks do not generally care for making or granting these loans. The reason for this is because the bank is putting up most or all of the up-front money for you to set yourself up in business. So, if your loan request is for venture capital, be ready to have some collateral for the bank. Normally, a bank will ask for some kind of security other than something like inventory, equipment, or contracts related to your business. It might be a good idea to meet with a business financial consultant to look over your business plan before approaching a bank. Should you not care to pay a financial consultant's fee, then lay out your business plan in advance and then take it to a banker and ask for their advice. Be sure to start slowly so as not to indicate that you are there for a large business loan. Likewise, play on the ego of the banker and use the right psychology when you want to make your loan request later on in the discussion. Make sure your business loan is realistic and ask for more than you really need. Let's say you need $25,000.00 dollars, ask for $30,000.00 and let the banker back the loan request down to $25,000.00 and yes, bankers will do this, but you will still have the funding you originally needed.

Banks are in business just like any other business, so be sure to shop around to find a bank that meets your needs. Think about banks like you would shopping for a car, furniture, or appliances because you're basically doing the same thing when shopping for a loan. The money that you save can be a large return for a few hours of work on the phone or by making personal contacts. People seeking larger loans may think that their time is too valuable to shop for loans, but the cost in points alone can be as much as five or six points between different banks. On a loan of a $150,000.00 dollars, this can equate to $9,000.00 dollars saved and on a $250,000.00 dollar loan, one could save as much as $15,000.00 dollars just in points alone for a few hours of work. If, on the other hand, you are making five-hundred or a thousand dollars an hour, you can afford to let someone else do the work for you.

WISHING YOU GOOD LUCK AND

HAPPY SHOPPING

NEGOTIATING

In's and Out's

THE FOLLOWING NEGOTIATING INFORMATION WILL NOT ONLY BE WORTH THE ENTIRE COST OF THIS BOOK, BUT IT WILL ALSO BE SOMETHING THAT YOU CAN USE FOR THE REST OF YOUR LIFE TO SAVE AND MAKE YOU THOUSANDS OF DOLLARS WHEN YOU ARE BUYING OR SELLING ANYTHING!

THIS INFORMATION IS COMPLIMENTS OF

Mark S. Kovach

SECTION 2

NEGOTIATING IN'S AND OUT'S

How to Negotiate on Anything

As I sit here pondering the above statement, I am trying to think of something that is not negotiable in this world and beyond. As far as the world as we know it is concerned, I really can't think of anything that can't be negotiated. However, if there is a heavenly world out there beyond our world, then I can think of several things that would not be negotiable. For example, I know that God's work—the Holy Bible, heaven, natural occurrences, etc.—are not negotiable. I know that the Scriptures in the Holy Bible are not negotiable (this was contributed by my wife). I know that one's infilling by the Holy Spirit cannot be negotiated. I know that the universe, with its stars and planets, is not negotiable. I know that natural disasters and occurrences like tornadoes, earthquakes, rain, wind, snow, day, and night are not negotiable. However, other than the above mentioned things, everything is negotiable in our world of retail sales. Therefore, the two rules I am about to give you can be used in nearly every aspect of your life.

RULE # 1

EVERYTHING IS NEGOTIABLE!

RULE # 2

REFER TO RULE # 1

NEGOTIATING GUIDELINES

Basically, as with everything else in this world, there are guidelines that you need to understand before you start a negotiation.

You must learn to enter all negotiations with a win-win-win thought process in mind.

You must know and identify what you want.

You should have a good idea of what the fair market value is concerning anything that you want to negotiate on.

You must be willing to give and take.

You must have financial capability.

You must accumulate as much factual information concerning what you want to negotiate on ahead of time.

You must be willing to ask for what you want or you will not even get started in the negotiation process.

You must be willing to walk away from any transaction.

You must be objective.

You must have patience.

You must learn to relax and appear as though your ability to negotiate is nothing more than an everyday routine.

You must learn to analyze people and situations as quickly as possible.

You must never appear to be doubtful or hesitant.

You must learn to trade off.

You must learn to become an expert at developing alternatives.

The Win-Win-Win Situation

**Keep in mind that when you start a
negotiation, you want a win-win-win situation.
In other words, this means that you will win,
the other person will win, and the company,
store manufacturer, vendor, or any other
entity will also win. Now, you may be
wondering, *if this is the case, how can anyone
win and yet still have a win-win-win situation?*
Simple!**

Allow me to explain some basic facts to keep in mind when it comes to negotiating. I'll start with a monetary item. For every product that you would like to acquire, the seller must have a certain built-in profit structure. The only question a seller has in that situation is, how much of a profit? All products or commodities must have a sufficient profit structure surrounding them to ensure that everyone will benefit if the buyer makes the purchase. This includes the seller's place of business, as well as the employees. This is otherwise referred to as overhead or the cost of doing business.

As an example, let's consider the purchase of a car. First of all you have a seller (private or commercial) who has an asking price. However, what you may not know is that the seller has two more prices in mind, the seller's wanting price and the seller's accepting price. Likewise, buyers have three prices in mind. This may sound a little strange, but some buyers actually have the asking price in mind as their offering price, and in fact, these buyers will usually end up paying the asking price. However, most buyers will have an offering price, a wanting price, and a paying price.

Now, let's view a win-win-win situation. The seller starts off with his best asking price and the buyer starts off with his best offering price. Whether or not the buyer is aware of it, he has just started negotiating. In turn, the seller becomes realistic, understanding that he will not receive his best wanting price because the buyer's best wanting price is still below the seller's best wanting price. The seller then informs the buyer of the price that he is willing to sell the car for, or the seller's accepting price.

Let's look at your first lesson in the art of negotiating. The seller has just indicated to the buyer what his accepting price will be, but don't believe him! As with every negotiation transaction that I have been involved with, the seller always has a rock-bottom or final accepting price. The buyer now indicates his paying price, or the price that he is willing and able to pay for the car. At this point, one of two things will occur: (1) the buyer will make the deal and everyone will be happy, or (2) neither party will conclude the transaction. Why might the latter occur? Because it is not a win-win-win situation.

If you are dealing with a commercial car dealership, there may not be a sufficient profit in the transaction or a sufficient incentive from the car manufacturer for the seller to cover his overhead expenses. Likewise, there may not be a sufficient profit for the private-party seller in the event that he has to pay off an existing loan balance or have sufficient money left over to make a down payment on another vehicle. However—and this is a very important point to remember—the buyer needs to realize that this is the point in his negotiation at which he can make a final offer in order to consummate the transaction! Unfortunately, it is at this point in the negotiation that most people would walk away because they have become upset or frustrated, feeling that they have not been treated fairly by the seller or that the seller does not want to do business with them. This is not true!

At this point in the negotiation, the seller is trying to tell the buyer what his rock-bottom or final accepting price will be for the transaction to be consummated. As the buyer, you must be in a position to either accept the seller's rock-bottom price, realizing that the deal will not go any further, or be willing to ask for additional concessions, such as an additional 25 percent discount on accessories, for which most dealerships will offer 10 percent. Both of you might settle for 15 percent if that is what it takes to close the transaction. Otherwise, you must be willing to walk away from the transaction!

Know and Identify What You Want

Learning the negotiating technique is not difficult. So why don't we negotiate? Simple: because we don't know what we want, and when we finally realize what we want, we usually end up paying the full price. Notice I said *usually*. This is because I personally never pay the full price for anything because I know what I want before I decide to make a purchase or a commitment. More importantly, I know what I am willing to pay to get what I want, and if my offer is not enough, I simply walk away and go elsewhere.

In the event that you gain nothing more out of this information, remember this: a product is only worth what someone is willing to pay for it! Allow me to rephrase this for clarification. Any product is only of value to the person who makes the purchase, and the price paid is the value to that person and that person only!

Knowing and identifying exactly what you want before you attempt to negotiate will afford you the opportunity to search the marketplace to learn what different prices are being quoted for the same product. The more knowledge that you can accumulate concerning the product that you would like to purchase, the better your negotiating position will be when you are ready to negotiate. In order to become a good negotiator, you must understand that there is more to closing a transaction than just being right. You have to learn to develop the insight to look beyond what most people are concerned about and to eliminate any possibility of tunnel vision, which the majority of people have been taught since birth. In other words, know what you want, and try to think outside of the box!

Know or Learn About the Market Value

Regardless of what you want to purchase, know or learn what the current market value is for that particular product. This means that whether you are considering buying a bicycle for yourself or the kids, carpet for your home, fixtures, clothing, diamonds, jewelry, home additions, a home loan—you name it—knowing what the current market value is will place you way ahead of the other person in the negotiating process.

What does it take to learn about the market value of any given product? No less than three inquiries. Depending on the price of the product, as many as five to ten or more inquiries may be needed. As a rule, I will only start to negotiate on a product priced from $1,000 to $5,000 after having made a minimum of three inquiries in the marketplace. For products priced from $5,000 up to $25,000, I will make anywhere from five to ten inquiries before deciding to negotiate. For any product priced above $25,000, I will make a minimum of ten inquiries, and then I will incorporate time (as in hours, days, weeks, or months) before making a decision to negotiate. Why? Because I want to know what the market value is as well as what the price fluctuations are in the current marketplace.

Once I have obtained this information, I will then decide the price I would like to purchase the product for as well as what I would be willing to pay. Unless I was willing to make those inquiries, I would never have any idea what the product would be worth on the open market. Not knowing better, I (like everyone else) would end up paying the full market price when

I could have saved a considerable amount of hard-earned money had I simply taken the time to research the market.

By learning the art of negotiating, the average person can save hundreds and thousands of dollars throughout his or her lifetime, and can become a successful negotiator. Nevertheless, with knowledge and skillful negotiations, anyone can learn to gain the leading edge in the negotiating process. As a negotiator, you will need the ability to develop and use every bit of knowledge, experience, and information you have gained thus far in your lifetime, which will place you above the rest of the crowd. Moreover, each time you make a choice to buy something, you will be doing so because you have negotiated the value and benefits that you want to receive.

Give and Take

Once you have decided that what you want is really what you want and you have researched the marketplace, you should have a better-than-average idea of the true value of the product that you would like to purchase. Now you should be ready to negotiate. Negotiating is fun, but being effective at it is an art. The negotiating techniques mentioned in the beginning of this section will not only help you appear more confident and perform accordingly, but practicing these techniques will also allow you to improve your concentration and alertness during the negotiating process. Remember: never lose sight of your objective. As a negotiator, you should remain calm and appear as though using your ability to negotiate is an everyday event. As you continue to practice, using your negotiating skills will then become as normal as saying your name when you introduce yourself.

In order for negotiations to be effective, you must understand the concept of give and take. Effective negotiations will convert your knowledge, experience, and information into dollar savings. Your ability to become an effective negotiator will depend on your ability to give and take in the negotiating process. The word *give* in this sense does not mean that you are to give away your rights, freedom, enjoyment, or money. On the contrary, in the art of negotiating, the word *give* means knowing what is right, fair, and equitable and placing yourself in your opponent's position.

The word *take* in this sense does not mean that you are to rip your opponent apart, show no mercy, or show no consideration or empathy. In the art of negotiating, the word *take* means knowing when to seek an alternative, concede to a valid point, restructure the offer, or be prepared to walk away until you have had the time to reconsider your position as well as that of your opponents. Once you have learned and understand the concept of give and take, you will be on your way to becoming an extremely effective negotiator. As you build confidence, your negotiating abilities will continue to improve and advance.

In the above two scenarios, you have and maintain the same common denominator, that is nothing more than a tool, which is money. If you think, and use money as a tool, you will be able to manipulate just about everything and anything you want or desire in your lifetime.

Financial Capability and Asking for What You Want

Never enter a negotiating process without having the financial capability to follow through with the transaction. A good negotiator may spend hours, days, weeks, months, or years negotiating for some particular item, but if he or she did not have the financial capability to follow through with the transaction, it would be a complete waste of time, money and energy. If you negotiate and you get what you want, you must be prepared and have the financial capability to close the transaction. The only time the above statement does not apply is in the event that you are out practicing your negotiating techniques. Incidentally, when you think you are ready to go out and practice negotiating, the best places to practice happen to be the hardest places to deal with, such as car dealerships, carpet and flooring dealers, large retail outlets, furniture companies, and building and plumbing supply companies. Even though you may not get what you want, the negotiating experience you gain will be invaluable, and the continued practice will only help sharpen your negotiating skills. Caution: Even though you may make some ridiculous requests while you are practicing negotiating, be careful not to get so caught up in the process that your opponent goes along with your request, and you end up in a situation in which you have to perform or you can never show your face in the area again. When you are out practicing your negotiating techniques, be sure to negotiate on an item that you know you will never be able to get your price on so as not to place yourself in an embarrassing and awkward position.

On the other hand, when you are serious about acquiring an item, be sure to ask for what you want and be specific;

otherwise you will never get what you really want. For example, let's say you want to buy a car. Be sure to ask for everything you want on that particular car and then ask for additional items that you don't want or even need on the car before you begin to negotiate on the final price. Why? Simple: making concessions by giving up certain items you asked for, but really don't want or need, will make the car salesperson feel guilty, which in turn will give you a much better shot at getting the price you want to pay for the car. Remember the give-and-take scenario? Well, in this situation asking for more than you want or need allows you the ability to take what you do want and give back what you really didn't want in the first place—but your opponent doesn't know what you are doing or thinking, as he or she just wants to make the deal if at all possible.

One thing about cars that everyone should remember is that buying any car is always a losing proposition because of depreciation. Car dealerships and manufacturers have been ripping off the general public for generations. As an example, let's look at a typical car transaction. Let's say the manufacturer is offering a family-and-friends discount of $2,000 in addition to the dealership's $1,500 discount if you purchase in a particular month. The average car on the market today runs around $30,000 out the door (OTD), so if we were to subtract the total incentives of $3,500 off the sticker price of $30,000, we could see that you would be able to purchase this car for only $26,500. Not bad? This is a total rip off! Even with the added manufacturer's discounts, people are only getting approximately a 12 percent discount, and if you were to drive off the dealer's car lot and immediately drive back on and request your money back, the dealer would only give you approximately $20,100 for the brand-new, discounted car.

When any car clears the dealer's car lot, the price drops by one-third, or 33 percent. This immediate depreciation rate is a figure all dealers use to calculate a repurchase, assuming the car is immediately returned to the dealer's car lot.

Therefore, when you are out negotiating for a new car, you should always start at the 30 percent mark in an attempt to get a 25 percent discount, and you should never go below a 20 percent discount if at all possible. Only once in my lifetime have I been able to get a full 30 percent discount on a new car. However, I have been able to get 25 percent most of the time, and I have never bought a car at less than a 20 percent discount. In other words, I would normally buy the above $30,000 car for between $22,500 (a 25 percent discount) and $24,000 (a 20 percent discount). If the car dealer insists that he or she will not be able to make any money by selling the car at a 20 percent or 25 percent discount, don't believe a word of it, even if he or she is willing to show you the purchase invoice. Ask the dealer to show you the manufacturer's invoice and not the dealership's made-up invoice, where they add on to the manufacturer's invoice.

Most car salespersons will normally avoid showing you the manufacturer's invoice if they can get away with it, or they will avoid the question by misdirecting the conversation in an attempt to get you to buy at the dealership invoice price. Don't buy it and insist on seeing the manufacturer's invoice and/or inform the dealership that X amount of dollars is all that you are willing to pay for the car, and then shut up! Why? For he or she who speaks first will lose in the negotiating process. I have even gone outside and waited for the dealer to make the first response, because it put me back in the driver's seat, so to speak. Likewise, when the dealer comes back with a response, don't give him a response right away, but rather take your time and tell him that you will have to think over the offer. Now, after you have taken some time to think it over, and if you believe that the offer does not meet with your expectations, tell the dealer that you will get back to him after you have had time to check with other dealers, and then slowly walk away from the offer. Why? Simple: Because should your offer for the car be within reason, the salesperson will inform the sales manager that you are going to another dealer. I can guarantee you that at that time someone from the dealership will catch you before you can get to your car and drive off.

This is the time in the negotiation process where you must maintain your composure and stand firm with your offer. Let the dealer squirm for a while, while you just listen to what he has to say and never agree with him or even nod your head on anything he is asking or saying—these questions and statements are known as little closes, a technique used to get you to the final closing. After all is said and done and you believe that you have negotiated your best deal, close the transaction. On the other hand, if you still believe that the dealership has not done what they can to meet your offer price, walk away and go to another dealership and start negotiating again—only this time you will be armed with information from the previous dealership that will give you the edge when you start negotiating for the same car. The trick here is to take the best price the previous dealer gave you, knock off another $2,000 or $3,000, and inform the new dealer that this is the best price that the previous dealer was able to offer you. But tell the new dealer that if a better deal could be struck, you would be happy to do business with their dealership. Again, shut up at this point, for he or she who speaks first loses.

Provided that you have the time, patience, and stamina, you will find out what you can really purchase the car for, as the new dealership will bend over backward trying to meet or beat the previous dealership's offer. Caution: A typical dealership response will be to ask you to get the offer in writing from the previous dealership. Don't fall for this tactic; instead, start laughing and say, "Sure, like the previous dealership would be willing to put their best offer in writing so we could go elsewhere and shop for a better deal? Would your dealership do the same? I seriously doubt it! So, either I can do business with your dealership, or I can go back and do business with the previous dealership. It doesn't make much difference to me because I only want to buy the car from the dealership offering the best pricing." Again, shut up at this point! This is when you can just kick back and relax and let the dealer come up with his best deal.

When the dealer comes back and gives you his so-called best offer, you can accept the offer, reject the offer, or take his best offer and go to another dealership and start negotiating all over again. Depending on the amount of time you are willing to invest, along with the amount of money you want to save, you can negotiate as many times as you want to.

As an example, I once went to a total of five different dealerships over five consecutive weekends before I finally made a deal to buy a particular SUV that I wanted, and I ended up getting a 22 percent discount off the sticker price, excluding the dealership's add-on pricing. This process of negotiating can be used on anything that you might be inclined to purchase. Going from one dealer to another with the same merchandise will always give you better insight as to what you will eventually be able to purchase the item for in the open marketplace.

Thinking on Your Feet

In order to become a great negotiator, you must have the ability to think on your feet. Over the years I have negotiated with many different kinds of people on all sorts of things—cars, boats, homes, land, printing materials, clothing, etc.—and the one thing that seems to stop most people from negotiating is that they don't enjoy conflict or are afraid they may get caught up in a rapid-fire question-and-answer situation that they wouldn't know how to handle, which includes my wife Joan! Then again, there are those people who just don't have any idea that one can negotiate on anything in this world and are willing to pay the asking price, just like my wife Joan before she met me. However, contrary to popular belief, negotiating can and will save you hundreds of thousands of dollars over your lifetime if you learn how to do it.

In the beginning of any negotiation process, each person is sizing up his or her opponent, and the process will usually proceed slowly until one or the other opponent finds a weakness in the other, at which time that person will concentrate on that weakness. The primary weakness that I have observed over my years of negotiating with people is their inability to think on their feet in a rapid-fire question-and-answer situation. This is how it works: First come the introductions; next the feeling-out process; next the process of finding out if the people negotiating know what they really want, determining if they can afford whatever it is they are negotiating for, and determining whether they are willing to trade or willing to give and take.

Once the above information has been assessed, and just when the buyers involved believe that they are going to be able to negotiate their deal, this is the time the salesperson starts rapidly firing questions at their opponents. The goal in this situation is to continue to ask questions as fast as possible, avoiding the answers and attempting to place the buyers in an uncomfortable situation by making them feel guilty or as though they would be taking the food off the dealer's table and the clothes off the dealer's children's backs. Now, if you are a beginner at negotiating, you need to avoid a rapid-fire question-and-answer situation, and the best way to do this is to simply ask your opponent to restate the first question, even if he is already on their third or fourth question. This technique is used by attorneys in a court of law all the time, and your attorney should teach you how to handle this situation, which is the same way I had to learn the hard way. You must slow your opponent down and off track as fast as you can. As time goes on and your negotiating knowledge and abilities continue to increase, handling a rapid-fire question-and-answer situation will become second nature because you will have learned how to think on your feet in order to handle it.

Trading Off or Developing Alternatives

One of the great advantages of negotiating is having the ability to trade off or develop alternatives during the negotiating process. If you remember the section entitled *"Financial Capability and Asking for What You Want,"* you will recall that I showed you how to ask for more than you want or need when negotiating the purchase of a car. Using this same scenario, let's say you asked for a six-CD changer, an MP3 player, upgraded wheels, a special roof rack, and a towing package including all the special wiring. You really don't want or need these things, but if the deal is negotiated properly, you would be willing to take these items. Your salesperson goes out of the room to see the sales manager in an attempt to get you the best price for your new car. This process can take anywhere from fifteen minutes to forty-five minutes or more, depending on how long they want you to squirm around in their little office before they think you are ready to leave the dealership. Suddenly your salesperson shows up with a big smile on his face and says, "Congratulations! The price of your new car will be [X], and the monthly payments will only be [Y], and the car has everything you wanted." However, instead of offering your negotiated price for the car, the salesperson gives you a price that is way out of line.

When you hear this news, you will normally think that you have been hit upside your head with a sledgehammer and that everything you have been negotiating on went in one of the salesperson's ears and out the other. This is the point when most people will walk away from the dealership or pay the quoted price. But this is not so for the professional negotiator, as this is the time when all your abilities, knowledge, and skills come into play. The real negotiation is about to begin. At this time you should inform your opponent that there seems to be a considerable difference between what you are willing to buy the car for and what the dealership wants you to pay for the car. Just ignore the surprised look that comes over the face of your salesperson, and begin to give back or trade off and develop alternatives in exchange for a better price for the car.

Inform the salesperson that as much as you would like to have the six-CD changer, you will have to settle for a regular CD player if he is willing to lower the price and downgrade the radio system. Likewise, as much as you really want the MP3 player, ask how much they will knock off the price if you give it up. The upgraded wheels are great, but ask how much can be saved if standard wheels are substituted. Tell the dealer that though you really need the roof rack, you will have to forego buying it because you can't afford it, then ask how much will be saved without the roof rack. Besides trading off, do you see what we are doing to the salesperson? We are taking our time and making not only the immediate salesperson feel guilty, but we are also making the invisible opponent (the sales manager) feel guilty. Each time you trade off something, make sure the salesperson goes back to the sales manager for confirmation. The more your opponent has to go back and forth, the better your chances are of getting exactly what you wanted in the first place as far as the price of the car is concerned.

Likewise, having the ability to develop alternatives is just as important as trading off when negotiating. Using the same scenario as above, when the negotiating situation seems to come to a point where no one is willing to continue to give and take, developing alternatives comes into play.

For example, let's say you are getting very close to getting the car you want at the price you want by trading off, but there still remains a difference of, say, $2,000 or $3,000. What do you do? Come up with alternatives, such as stating to your salesperson, "I might be willing to accept the car at the price you have quoted us, provided we can get a 25 percent discount on accessories or a 25 percent discount on parts or free car washes any time we bring the car in for service as long as we own the car." Ask for the same regarding any other services that the dealership can offer to continue to get your business after the sale. Now, you might get a 10 percent discount on parts and a 15 to 20 percent discount on any additional accessories you may want sometime in the future, but remember, every time you buy parts or accessories at a negotiated discount, you will be closing the gap on the sales price of the car over any given period during which you own the car and do business with the same dealership.

One final thought in dealing with car dealerships: Don't think for one minute that you are taking the food and clothing away from your opponent, and don't believe any dealer who tells you that they paid the manufacturer's suggested retail price (MSRP) for the vehicle, as this is outright ludicrous. Think about this for a minute: When times get hard and retail sales drop off and a recession might be on the way, it is not unusual for car dealerships to start cutting their prices in order to attract business. When things get really tough and a recession has taken hold of our society, you see car dealerships advertising and selling vehicles at half of the MSRP sticker price and not at the dealership's total add-on prices. I am currently living in Texas, and as I am writing this book, day after day we see and hear the car dealerships advertising to sell their vehicles for half off the MSRP. Therefore, if it is possible for a car dealership to sell a vehicle for half the price indicated on the MSRP and still be able to make money, you as a potential buyer should not be too concerned with the idea that you may be taking advantage of any dealership as they have been gouging the general public for years.

All of the above negotiating information has been used and tested again and again by me, and it never ceases to amaze me that people do not negotiate when they know that they have absolutely nothing to lose and everything to gain in the form of dollar savings. Nevertheless, this negotiating information can be used for just about anything a person may desire, keeping in mind that the end result will be a

WIN-WIN-WIN SITUATION!

REMEMBER,

SUCCESS IS NOT AN ACCIDENT

AND

WHEN ALL ELSE FAILS,

NEGOTIATE!

Wishing you good fortune, and God bless you in all of your endeavors.

Sincerely,

Mark S. Kovach

Author

Other Books By Mark Kovach

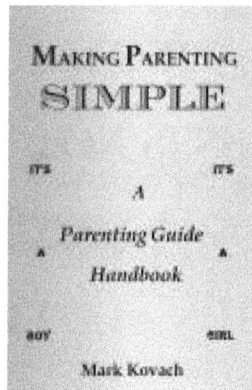

Available at Amazon, Kindle & other Book Stores

Making Parenting Simple Handbook

By Mark Kovach

The basic concept of Making Parenting Simple Handbook is to train your child while they are developing in the womb or as soon after birth up until the age of 5 or 6 that are the most critical years of a child's life. The book includes chapters on how to protect your child, especially, girls under the age of 21 and a whole lot more of relevant parental information concerning older children.

Home Buying and Financing 101

By Mark Kovach

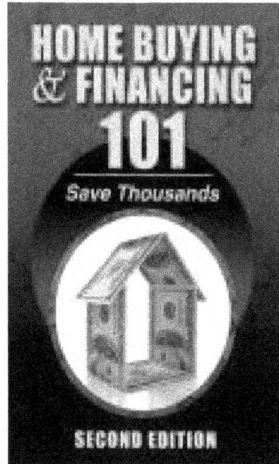

This book Home Buying & Financing 101 Second Edition is a **MUST READ** for anyone who may be considering Buying a Home and Understanding the Financial details and implications of financing their new home which was originally written and designed for the Loan Officers and Real Estate Agents and now for the general public which includes new updates and subjects such as the Reverse Mortgage and how to never lose your home plus other information that was designed for the benefit of the general home-buying public.

How Anyone Can Retire: Living Large...

By Mark Kovach

HOW ANYONE CAN

RETIRE

Living Large on Pennies

MARK KOVACH

How Anyone Can Retire: Living Large on Pennies is a no-nonsense guide to prepare yourself for the retirement that you have worked for so hard to enjoy. By following the steps in the second half of the book that Mark Kovach and his wife took to become well off, you can accelerate your departure from the daily grind — and remain in retirement indefinitely.

www.ingramcontent.com/pod-product-compliance
Lightning Source LLC
Chambersburg PA
CBHW031730210326
41520CB00042B/1748